ANTICIPATING DISRUPTION

Boards should ask:
What If...?, not just Why...?

By

Roger Parry

Copyright © Roger Parry 2021

The most successful companies have boards which anticipate future events rather than becoming bogged down in governance and reporting. The best boards ask: "What if...?", not just "Why...?"

A board of directors combines the skills of executives and non-executives. It should be the forum for discussion to prepare a company to respond to disruptive events – good and bad.

Boards must serve the demands of a wide range of stakeholders. The days are past of running a business purely to create value for shareholders. Companies are now judged on the degree to which they are good corporate citizens. Under this pressure some boards get too focused on regulatory compliance and ESG (Environmental, Social and Governance) and fail to ensure their organization thrives by anticipating future disruption.

Contents

OBJECTIVE OF THIS BOOK	**5**
CONTEXT FOR THE BOOK	**11**
Systemic Shocks	11
WWW: What Went Wrong for consumer publishing?	17
WHAT ARE BOARDS FOR?	**25**
Maximising Shareholder Value	28
The Board Balancing Act	29
Stakeholder Surrogates	30
Board Composition	31
Diversity of Thought	34
The Role of Executive Directors	36
Good Boards and Bad Boards	37
Progressive and Regressive Boards	39
ASKING WHAT IF…?	**42**
Risk Register Rituals	43
Being Curious	44
False Assumptions	47
Understand your own economics	51
Competitors	55
Customers	57
Substitutes	58
Suppliers	60
New Entrants	61
Demographics	63
Environment	64
Technology	65
Legislation And Regulation	67
Employees	68
MAKING IT HAPPEN	**70**
CONCLUSIONS	**74**
Acknowledgements	78

OBJECTIVE OF THIS BOOK

This book promotes the proposition that the most effective boards of companies (both commercial and not-for-profit) anticipate future disruption – both good and bad. They should spend more time on this rather than being too focused on monitoring financial performance, regulation and governance. Budgeting and planning are largely an extrapolation of recent performance and much of the input to these processes is retrospective analysis of financial metrics - trying to understand why the most recent results look the way they do. This is a necessary part of a board's task but the real value comes from directors asking themselves "What If...?" more than "Why did...?"

The board brings together executives and non executives in the role of directors and is the ideal forum to discuss how an organization must change to thrive. A "progressive" board is thinking about the future, a "regressive" board is trying to explain the past to manage the present.

The executives who run an organization, quite rightly, worry about the here and now and are rewarded for delivering immediate and short-term results. But the board, which normally includes some of those executives sitting as directors, is the place where the "what's next...?" discussions should occur. Boards in the UK have a legal duty to "promote the success" of their company in a broad sense and to do this effectively they should be able to not just issue accurate financial reports but must anticipate events, take a view about changes in their operating environment, have contingency plans and look around corners for discontinuities.

Boards are a collection of individuals, ideally, from a broad range of backgrounds with a wide set of skills. They come together for the specific purpose of providing oversight of an organization and there is a natural tendency to want to base decisions on hard numbers which can be audited and then compared to budget projections and past performance. They are also expected to focus on governance issues such as remuneration, diversity and environment where success tends to be defined by targets set by third parties. Directors have a legal responsibility to make certain their organization complies with the law and regulations and that financial reports are accurate, but they must also try to ensure they are thinking ahead.

It is often more intellectually comfortable for the group that makes up the board to focus on their reporting duties which are broadly fact-based rather than indulge in speculation about the unknown. But the most successful organizations, which thrive in rapidly changing times, are those which put more emphasis on the future than the past. These are governed by a progressive board.

Our lives are shaped by the discussions of people who sit on boards. Boards control companies - private, public and not-for-profit. Commercial businesses, charities, hospitals, schools, government departments are all normally run by a board. These groups of people make decisions which affect us all. But board members should ask themselves exactly what they are trying to achieve. Is it reporting or performance ? What should be their objectives as a board? What does success look like?

Boards have developed, over centuries in all nations and cultures, to provide control. They try to ensure that an organization, whatever its purpose, is accountable to the people who own shares in it, supply it, buy from it and work for it. They provide accountability. But a board is just a group of individuals who have been given collective responsibility. Each group is different. There are no hard and fast rules about the size of boards, the frequency of meetings or the way they are run. Each board is *sui generis*. Each group of directors develops its own culture, norms, style, and cadence.

This book is not about the micro mechanics of making boards work. It will not discuss the best way to keep minutes or present board papers. There are no "handy hints for first-time chairmen." No detailed analysis of Section 172 of the UK's 2006 Companies Act – although it does come up a few times. This book promotes the argument that the most important task of a board is making judgements about the future of its organization. Anticipating events and making contingency plans. Outsmarting the competitors, adapting to changes and ensuing the organization is well placed. It is about asking questions about what might happen, more than what has happened. This book argues that, ultimately, performance is more important than governance and that the most critical part of performance is making the right judgements about, and contingency plans for, future uncertainties.

Anticipating Disruption is not a book of management theory. It is mostly derived from my own experiences on corporate boards both commercial and not-for-profit. It is not specific to any one industry or sector. The need to get the balance right between governance and performance and to make time think about, discuss and plan for the future is paramount whether the measure of success is shareholder value, patient care, good schooling or great theatre.

In recent years there has been a switch of emphasis away from the focus on creating shareholder value and pure financial performance to what was once called CSR (Corporate Social Responsibility) and is now termed ESG (Environmental, Social and Governance). These developments are both welcome and necessary as boards recognise that organizations do not exist in a vacuum. Companies are part of wider society and must play a responsible social role. It is not just virtue signalling to try to do the "right thing". ESG awareness is good for business as well as assuaging political , social and environmental pressures. Customers and employees, let alone regulators and campaigners, increasingly demand good ethical practices which usually lead to good financial performance. But some boards do seem to have lost the plot. In their anxiety to tick ESG boxes they forget their main purpose - which is to see their organization survive and thrive. Their collective task is not just to win points in ESG audits but to think about long-term success.

Nearly all boards combine full-time executives, whose task is the run the organization (the management) with non-executives (appointed by owners, shareholders, government etc) to provide oversight of the executive's actions and to give the organization its own "personality" and accountability in law. All directors have the same legal obligations. Collectively the directors are responsible for the conduct of the entity.

At the risk of oversimplification, the executive group – who will normally meet regularly in a "management committee" or something similar - look, in detail, at day-to-day performance. Those same executives, or some of them, will also attend the board which, if it is run properly, has the luxury of thinking longer-term. The board should be the venue where the general experience and external perspective of the non-executives and the operating knowledge and specific experience of the management combine to map out the future path. However, some boards get bogged down in overly meticulous monitoring of performance metrics; and others can spend hours enjoyably, but rather pointlessly, discussing macro-economic and social issues more suited to a post-graduate seminar. Both extremes make the board dysfunctional. Directors need to keep themselves focused on the task at hand – having a common view about what happens next.

In writing this book I have been heavily influenced, possibly "scarred" by the experience of having been chairman of two UK-based publishing companies for most of the first decade of the current century. I was, simultaneously chairman of both Johnston Press (2001 to 2009) which ran some 300 regional and local newspapers and Future (2001 to 2011) which owned 100 plus specialist magazines. Both, in the early 2000s, made most of their money from selling printed advertising and were reliant on selling copies via newsagents. Both felt the full force of the arrival of the internet during my tenure. Future has gone on to thrive and at the time of writing is a stock market darling worth more than £ 2 billion. Johnston, as a company, basically collapsed in 2018 with debts of more than £200m and was recently sold for £10 million. The lessons of these two divergent trajectories have been very instructive for me. I have written them up in more detail in the "WWW- What Went Wrong" chapter, but the headline comment is that the board of Future saw the internet as an opportunity to be grasped whilst at Johnston they saw it as a threat to be deflected. One board was good at seeing around corners the other was not. One was "progressive" the other "regressive" As I was chairman of both the experience has demonstrated to me the value of the old adage that "we learn from our mistakes."

I have been working as non-executive chairman for more than 20 years. I have chaired the board of seven publicly listed companies, four private ones and have been a director of some half a dozen others. I was also chairman of Shakespeare's Globe Trust a large not-for-profit charity. The ideas and observations in this book come from this direct experience. This is not an academic work of research or a journalistic investigation. This is one person's observations which I hope, being based on direct experience, will be a useful contribution to the discussion.

This is a short book – by design. It has one basic message that boards should be forward looking. There is a view amongst some publishers that to be credible a management book needs to weigh in at 300 plus pages and half a kilo. But in a digital age I think there is an argument for keeping a book short and "on message". There is a wealth of historical comment on the merits on brevity.

"I would have written a shorter letter, but I did not have the time"

It's a great quote with a disputed provenance. There are numerous candidates. In 1690 English philosopher John Locke said of one of his own, rather long, books

> "But to confess the truth, I am now too lazy, or too busy to make it shorter."

In 1750 American statesman Benjamin Franklin comments one of his own essays:

> "I have already made this paper too long, for which I must crave pardon, not having now time to make it shorter."

American humourist Mark Twain is widely credited with:

> "I didn't have time to write you a short letter, so I wrote you a long one."

But the earliest example is author Blaise Pascale who wrote (in French) in 1657 about one of his own letters:

> "I have made this longer than usual because I have not had time to make it shorter."

I think M Pascale must win the attribution game. So this book is, unapologetically, short with *kudos* to Blaise Pascale.

CONTEXT FOR THE BOOK

The next two sections provide context for the ideas in the rest of this book. Theses are brief notes on the big events – the *Systemic Shocks* – which companies and their boards have faced during my time in boardrooms over some 30 years. Then a chapter with details of the experiences I had when, simultaneously, chairing two UK-based publishing companies in the early 2000s. *WWW:What Went Wrong ?* explains how the two companies reacted in very different ways to the arrival of the internet.

Systemic Shocks

If all business was, "Business as Usual" – BaU, there is an argument that the conventional board would hardly need to exist. In circumstances where everything is predictable success is simply a matter of doing the same thing tomorrow that you did yesterday – perhaps just a bit more of it. In pure BaU the role of directors on a board is limited to monitoring, governance and oversight - making sure that the management do not do anything criminal and don't run off with the money. Almost an internal audit function.

However, the reality of organisational life is that, for most of the time, there is no such thing as BaU. At the macro level there are events such as banking crises, recessions, political changes, and pandemics. At a micro level senior employees get sick or quit, factories burn down, competitors launch a new product or customers change their behaviour.

Most systemic shocks cannot realistically be predicted and, by definition, are rarely company specific. Boards can and do maintain risk registers for the sort of things they know might go wrong for their own organizations. They can then put in place processes and plans so that when such a shock occurs the organisation is ready to react rapidly. An obvious example is disaster recovery around a collapse of IT storage . Alternative data resources and server capacity can be identified and held in reserve. If the worst happens a plan is in place.

System shocks catch nearly everyone by surprise. They were memorably described as "Black Swans" in a book of the same name in 2007 by Nassim Nicholas Taleb.[1] I was on boards throughout this period and was Chairman of several from 2001 onwards. In each case we asked a lot of questions about "can we survive". In retrospect I wish we had spent more time asking "how might we benefit from this and emerge in a better position

1987 Black Monday Crash

In early October 1987 variety of factors caused a lot of investors to want to sell equities in a hurry. From the middle of 1982 most of the world's large stock markets, in particular New York and London, had enjoyed a huge boom in share prices. Over the same period there was a great increase in the number of shares available to be traded and a significant growth in the use of financial derivatives which allowed people to take what amounted to gambling positions on their guesses about the direction of share prices movements. Added to this there had been the development of computer-based trading where the machine made orders to trade shares triggered, automatically, by price movements.

In the early weeks of October 1987 there was a general concern that the market had peaked, and people were looking to liquidate some of their portfolios to reduce their risks. In London a related

---

[1] *The Black Swan: The Impact of the Highly Improbable* Nassim Nicholas Taleb. 2007 Random House

factor was that on the Friday October 16th there had been an exceptional storm, literally a hurricane, which had resulted in the UK stock market being closed thus when it opened on the Monday morning there was additional uncertainty and a pent up demand.

With a combination of automated trading and panic selling share prices dropped by more than 20% in a day. The largest fall in stock market history – hence the name Black Monday. It took nearly 2 years until 1989 for share prices to recover their losses. However, the "real" economy: employment, manufacturing output, retail sales were largely unaffected.

Black Monday was a shock to investment professionals and a challenge to companies planning to issue shares to fund take-overs and mergers. It did cause recruitment and retention problems in organization where stock options were a big element of the remuneration package. But it turned out to be no more than a blip on a decade long boom of economic growth which was the backdrop to the far more damaging events of 1991/92.

1991/92 UK Recession

The 1980s had been a period of economic growth across the world. In the UK there was the so-called "Lawson boom" after Chancellor Nigel Lawson had encouraged rapid expansion of the British economy. But this led to high inflation, a big jump in house prices and high interest rates. In 1990 the UK joined the European Exchange Rate Mechanism (the ERM) which required the government to manage the exchange rate of the pound in a narrow band. Also, in 1990 Iraq invaded Kuwait leading to a sudden jump in oil prices. All these factors combined with problems with the savings and loans companies in the USA led to a rapid fall in consumer, business and investor confidence.

House prices collapsed, unemployment in the UK jumped to over 10% and many companies, unable to service debts with the new high bank rates, went bust. For 5 consecutive quarters the UK economy shrank. Unlike Black Monday the recession of 1990/91 did real damage to businesses and employment. It was a great time to buy a house or a company but a bad time to be looking for a job.

Recovery started in 1992 and there then followed a decade of boom which proved to be a golden age for business and entrepreneurs leading to the over exuberance of the 2001 internet melt down.

2001 Dot.Com Crash

A principle feature of the final years of the long boom of the 1990s was the rise of the so-called dot com stocks - companies which used the internet to create services. The euphoria around the potential of internet companies (correct as it turned out in the long-run) allowed a large number of unprofitable business with substantial cash outgoings to achieve very high share prices at a early stage of their development. The huge valuations based purely on the assumption of them having huge future potential. Perhaps the most famous was Amazon which listed its shares in 1997. Many hundreds of others (now long forgotten like Pets.com and Webvan) did the same. Business which served the internet economy such as telecommunications and software firms also enjoyed substantial share price gains. Boards planned on the basis that this was sustainable.

Many of the dot-com and technology stocks traded on the NASDAQ exchange in the USA – the index of which rose by 400% from 1995 to March 2000. In early April 2000 Microsoft lost a major court case against the US Government which accused it of monopolist practices. This combined with several negative press stories about dot.com valuations led to a sudden loss of confidence. What had been euphoria turned to panic and prices of technology and internet companies collapsed. Over the next couple of years the

NASDAQ dropped by nearly 80% and funding dot.coms became far more difficult. Amazon lost 90% of its value.

But as with Black Monday the damage to the real economy outside of internet start-ups was slight. It was a bad time to be looking for a job in Silicon Valley but for most people and businesses life went on as before. Amazon re-invented its business model and planned for a post-crash future. The 1990s economic boom was back on track until 2007 when reality caught up with the banking industry.

2007/09 Global Financial Crisis (the "GFC")

Over many years of the economic boom share prices had risen, house prices had risen and banks, particularly in America, had lent huge amounts of money to individuals and companies who could not really afford to take on the debt. Far too many people fancied themselves as property speculators. Stories emerged of nurses in Florida on US$30,000 a year who owned three homes with a multi-million-dollar mortgage. In the UK in September 2007 a small bank called Northern Rock, which had made very generous mortgage loans, had to be rescued by the Bank of England – it was an early sign of trouble to come. In the USA a huge bank, Bears Stearns, failed in March 2008 and September that year a real giant of the sector - Lehman Brothers - declared bankruptcy.

Governments around the world had to use many billions of dollars to prop up the banking system the mistakes of which now threated chaos in the real economy. For more than a year starting in 2008 the UK economy was in recession. Business collapsed. Jobs were lost.

The GFC left countries and companies in much greater level of debt but interest rates were brought down to extremely low level and stayed that way for more than a decade. Low interest rates have saved many a company from bankruptcy and helped the finances of governments who have borrowed unprecedented amounts of money. But the same low rates have led to very high share prices and created a relatively fragile economy which was ill prepared for a forecast and indeed arguably unforecastable highly infectious viral disease.

2020 Covid-19 Pandemic

Whether it started in October 2019 or March 2020 and whether it was caused by people in Wuhan eating bats or by a medical laboratory accident does not affect the economic impact. The UK government, in line with most others, decided to lockdown the country which forced many businesses to close or operate at dramatically reduced capacity. Most organizations would have had "pandemic" on their risk register, but I doubt many, if any, predicted the impact as having to shut up shop for nine months or more.

Indications are that the 2020 Pandemic will have a more lasting impact on society than the GFC or any prior recession and it is very unlikely that most boards either predicted the scale or had robust plans for dealing with the consequences. I am not aware of any organizations which had plans for what they would do if their staff were forced to work from home and in many cases their customers were banned for visiting their business for months on end.

But many of the effects of the Pandemic are things that would have happened anyway but over a few decades rather than a few months. Arguably companies should have had plans for what they would do if people turned their backs on conventional 9to5 office life and wanted to work from home and avoid commuting. Retailers and restaurant had already seen the trends towards home delivery – perhaps they should have been ready to move faster.

The underlying demands of environmental protection have made business travel look unattractive for some time and the enabling technologies of high-speed broadband and video conferencing have been developing fast. The work-from-home revolution was always on the cards. The pandemic just made it happen much faster than expected.

WWW: What Went Wrong for consumer publishing?

This section is about the long-term impact of the internet on two UK-based consumer publishing companies: Future and Johnston Press. I was chairman of both for nearly a decade in the 2000s. The different way the two boards behaved is, for me, an object lesson in why the message of *Anticipating Disruption* is important. Since I left the two companies have experienced notably divergent performance in a radically changed environment. One is now a stock market favourite, the other collapsed.

The World Wide Web was conceived of by Sir Tim Berners Lee in 1989. It started to have commercial applications in the mid 1990s. The Web did not come as a surprise to the boards of either Johnston or Future but the way their responded was a reflection of their corporate past and the nature of their boards.

In 2003 the global investment bank Merrill Lynch published a chart of the best performing media stocks in Europe by relative growth in market value. Future was top (65% better than the mean), Johnston Press was second (59% better). At the bottom was renown the Reuters (minus 63%) – seen as a likely internet loser and in the middle the highly successful Sky TV at plus 17%. It was a heady time for me to be chairman of both these leading consumer publishers. The great success of the share prices in 2003 was for different reasons – reasons which would ultimately determine their dissimilar destinies.

Johnston has been founded by the Johnston family in the late 1700s and by year 2000 the family still held a large proportion of the shares. I took over the Chair from Fred Johnston – becoming the first non-family Chairman in more than 200 years. In the early 2000s Johnston Press was a stock market darling. Its 2003 performance reflected the almost universal acclaim of investors, analysts, and media commentators. "JP," as it was known, ran highly profitable local newspapers and grew rapidly by buying more titles.

The business model of JP was seen by investors as nearly perfect. Its money came from classified advertising. Car dealers, estate agencies and big employers seeking staff. Motors, Property and Jobs – the "three rivers of gold." Each local newspaper was, in effect, a monopoly. If you wanted to sell a house in Falkirk, you paid for an advertisement in the *Falkirk Herald*. If you wanted to buy a house in Falkirk, you went to the newsagent and purchased a copy of the *Falkirk Herald*. Both sides of the transaction paid JP for the privilege of doing business with each other.

Johnston had listed on the stock exchange in 1988. It used its shares to acquire other titles and its earnings and share price just kept going up. Fred Johnston was known, fondly and respectfully, in the local newspaper world as the "widows' friend" as he often purchased titles from small family firms who no longer could keep them up when the patriarch died. Every time JP did a deal investors applauded. Its management team were widely praised as the best in the business. Just before the 2003 banking league table JP had acquired titles including the *Yorkshire Post* and the *Portsmouth News*. As Chairman it was my happy duty to get congratulatory calls from investors reminding me to pay our management well to ensure they did not leave.

Future's even more stellar relative share price performance in 2003 was for a very different reason. Future was two centuries younger than Johnston. It has been founded in 1985 on his kitchen table, literally, by journalist Chris Anderson who was early to see the growth in computers and computer games. His first title was *Amstrad Action* giving people ideas about how to get the most out of their home computers. He went to launch or buy tiles like *PC Gamer* and published the official magazine of all three main gaming platforms Nintendo, PlayStation, and X Box.

A resident of San Francisco and an early adopter of technology Chris really struck gold by launching *Business 2.0* which, in 1998, became THE in-house magazine of the growing dot.com boom. In 1999 it sold more than 2000 pages of advertising making tens of millions of dollars in sales and profits. Future was by this stage owned by private equity firm Apax who seized the moment of maximum internet hysteria to float the company on the London stock market. I joined the board at the time of that IPO to see the share price rocket and the company valued at over £ 1 billion. Future was lauded as the #1 magazine publisher in the vanguard of the internet economy. Drinking the new economy *Kool Aid* the business expanded at breakneck speed.

But the success of Future proved ephemeral. At its height, in early 2000, the company's shares traded at more than 60 times earnings as investors expect huge growth to come. Johnston by contrast was also worth in excess of a billion pounds but traded on a far less racy 10 times earnings. The Johnston's valuation reflected decades of successful performance. Future's was driven by the expectation of unlimited web-based wealth.

When the dot.com crash happed in late 2000 Future was caught in the headlights. Advertising revenues from the internet start-ups collapsed as dot.com companies which had been huge spenders in *Business 2.0* to promote themselves went to the wall. The Future business model was in ruins, confidence collapsed and so did the share price. Faced with big debts, unused but expensive office space and large redundancy costs Future had to do an emergency rights issue at 20 pence a share – a tiny fraction of its pre-crash price. Founder Chris Anderson, always the visionary, left the business to go onto to storied success as the owner of the conference company TED. I became Chairman of Future at that point to help to find a way out of the mess.

By 2002 the two Boards of Johnston and Future were in very different places – financially and mentally. Johnston was riding high as the threat of online classified seemed remote. *Autotrader* was still mostly a print publication. *Rightmove* was a tiny, private joint venture of a few estate agents. *Monster* and other online recruitment sites were just getting going. JP's EDIBTA margin – the analysts' key test of success – was over 30%. Top line growth was double digits. The shareholders simply wanted "more of the same". The share price was robust. The board was happy,

Future, by contrast, was feeling bruised and worried. A brutal cost cutting plan had brought the company back to profit. Debt was paid down and the stock market value staged a recovery bounce – hence the leadership of the Merrill Lynch table. But the board remained worried about the threat of internet and took little consolation from the recovered share price. They felt more challenging change was coming.

As Chairman of both it was a bizarre experience. Both boards hired consultants to help us plan for an internet future. Deloitte, Enders, KPMG, OC&C all made contributions to our thinking. A consistent message started to emerge that the technology of the web would undermine traditional media and that advertising revenue and content would go digital. Both boards had the same information. They reacted in very different ways.

The board of Johnston were for the most part very successful and highly respected businessmen. Mostly aged over 60. The Scottish establishment. They listened to all the advice and concluded the internet was a threat but that it was a longways off. They were reassured by the dot.com crash feeling it reduced the ability of start-ups to raise cash and reduced risk of disruption.

The board of Future was unconventional, much younger and included, for a few years, Elizabeth Murdoch. It saw the internet as an opportunity and considered the dot.com crash was a minor blip on the way to dramatic web-driven change.

Johnston's planning was based on fending off the digital threat and continuing to grow by acquiring conventional assets. Future planned on a digital future by seeking to exploit the new technology both in content creation and distribution. Different elements of the investment community supported both approaches. Johnston appealed to the traditionalists who wanted dividends and scale. Future was attractive to investment funds who thought big changes were underway and wanted to make a bet on Web 2.0. The board of each company was all too conscious of its shareholders' expectations. A few anecdotes illustrate the differences.

In 2003 I had a brief meeting with Jonathan Harmsworth who, in his early 30s had recently become the fourth Viscount Rothermere running his family publishing empire the Daily Mail group which included a lot of local newspapers and competed directly with Johnston Press. He told me had returned from San Francisco having met a man called Craig Newmark who was using the internet to give away classified advertising listings. Jonathan felt this was very bad news for local publishers dependent on classifieds. The next day I was chairing a JP board and reported the conversation. One of the long-standing directors remarked that "Jonathan was a young man and the young get overexcited by new things". He went on to say "Pubs and newsagents had been allowing classified advertising on notice boards for years and this would not be a problem"

In 2004 the 300 or so local titles of Johnston Press reached some 6 million weekly readers. As a result of a question at the board - suggested by one of our external consultants the executives were asked to find out how many of these readers were subscribers. It took a month to discover the answer which was there were fewer than 400,000 customers who paid a subscription and for whom we had an address – let alone an email address. Johnston had the classic local newspaper dilemma that most readers purchased copies, when they felt like it, from a newsagent for cash. The company had no real relationship with the vast majority of customers nor any idea who they were.

In the same year the then head of Google Europe Nikesh Arora agreed to come to talk the Future board about how he saw media developing. He stressed the need to have close relationship between the media owner and each specific reader. He introduced us to the concept of ARPU – Average Revenue per User and the notion of big data and relationships. He suggested the internet would overwhelm traditional publishers. The board left the meeting shocked and determined to react.

Future was already committed to being the publisher of niche titles which attracted specialist readers. "Media with Passion" was the corporate tag line. From about that time Future accepted traditional print and retail distribution was simply one route to market and one we, as a group, felt it was in rapid decline. The company invested heavily in digital and within a year it was the largest supplier of digital magazine content to the fast-growing Apple Store – no printing press involved.

Future saw that digital media was not simply the print magazine in another format. The company already published a successful product review title called *T3* (standing for Tomorrow's Technology Today). As befits a gadget magazine it was one of the first with its own web site. Many publishers would have made that site their digital offer. But Future wanted to experiment with pure online media and launched an e-commerce site called *TechRadar* which in some ways was a direct competitor to T3's digital offering. But because *TechRadar* made no attempt to be a magazine its format and content were ideally suited to the needs of digital native, online shoppers and it now regularly features in the lists of top 100 digital destinations.

By the time I stepped down as chairman at Johnston in 2009 the damage of classified migration was all too visible. The "rivers of gold" were running dry. Rightmove was booming. Autotrader was making the transition to digital (it ceased printing in 2013), the NHS and other big employers were advertising jobs on their own web sites. Google was starting to sell local advertising in a big way much to the delight of local plumbers , electricians and home owners. Faced with a dramatic collapse in advertising Johnston started multiple rounds of cost cutting which produced a downward spiral into eventual collapse.

At Future, by the time I left the company in 2011 it had made numerous early stage digital investments and the management team went on to brilliantly execute and expand on the digital strategy. Future is now worth around £ 2 billion - much more than at the height of the original dot.com boom.

So what are the lessons for this book. The elements of the internet economy: the digital distribution of content, the growth of subscriptions, the value of customer relationships and data, the inevitable migration of classified adverting to web sites were all just as visible to both boards. If I want to claim some credit for the success of the board at Future, I must accept equal blame for the board's role in the demise of Johnston.

I think it comes down to two things. Having the "only the paranoid survive mentality" of Andy Grove and looking at a more distant time horizon than the annual results. Johnston was hugely self-confident and widely praised. Future had had a corporate near-death experience the board was anxious. JP was focussed on next year's numbers. Future (living up to its name) talked about (we really did) what the consumer media industry would look like in the next decade.

Chris Anderson the founder of Future was telling the board for many months, before he left, that the traditional print magazine was dead in the water. It was not a popular message for our board, management or investors and he was far ahead of his time. But Chris's warning did shake the board out of any complacency and prepare the ground for a new approach. Future was ready to consider new ideas.

At Johnston the board was able to reminisce about how the company had survived two world wars and the Great Depression and this led to the sense that the internet was to be endured rather than embraced so the company doubled down by investing in the tried and tested.

The fundamental difference between Johnston and Future was that Future changed its business model to reflect what the board thought would happen whilst Johnston stuck to its guns. Future looked around the corner and anticipated disruption.

WHAT ARE BOARDS FOR?

As individuals we make numerous personal decisions about our lives, behaviour and finances. We decide, for ourselves, where we want to live, if we want to buy a particular product, spend money, save money or take out a loan. We set our own ethical and social standards. We might choose a vegetarian diet and be very active in recycling. We might prefer to eat meat and drive a gas guzzling car. As individuals we are self-governing. We accept our choices will effect how others see us. Boards are required to act in the same way for their company – which is, for all practical purposes, a "person" in law.

In early human society most organizations – farms and businesses - were owned and run by individuals and families. Ownership and management were vested in the same people. It was only when enterprises got bigger and outside investors put their capital at risk that new structures were needed to govern them.

 The idea of corporations. where groups of individuals clubbed together as shareholders to buy shares in an enterprise, has its roots in China in the first millennium. In Europe, there are examples of mills and mines (ventures which required up-front cash investments) as far back as the 1200s. The idea of corporations – joint stock companies - really got going in the 1600s to help fund overseas trading activities and gave rise to organizations like The East India Company and the Hudson's Bay Company.

The shareholders of these corporations were sometimes also employees and managers but increasingly they were not involved other than having the legal right to share in any dividends paid by the company. Even from these very early days a "company" was regarded in law, as if it were a person with its own rights and obligations. The company could sue and be sued. It could own things; it could employ people. It would not be strictly true to say shareholders "owned" it. They owned economic rights to a share of the wealth it created but in some ways the company owned itself – like a person. But it was run by its managers – the people who worked for it and this gave those individuals real power. The development of the corporation created the role of the professional manager and this in turn, created the so-called "agency problem" and it is this "agency problem" that the device of the corporate board, with its independent non-executives, seeks to solve. The problem being to ensure the agents – the paid managers - don't make decisions which benefit them more than they do the shareholders who put up the capital.

The board is there to ensure that the rights of all the various parties are respected. In the 18th and 19th centuries this mostly meant balancing the dividends of shareholders with the salary and perks going to the management but increasingly, in the 21st century boards are expected to stand-in for many other groups such as customers, employees, suppliers, regulators and environmental campaigners.

When people work together to invest in assets in pursuit of an agreed goal they have created an organization. The goal can be almost anything: Provide education services (a school), health services (hospital), sell products (a retailer) or make profits from investing (a hedge fund). It is an almost infinite list. As a broad distinction, organizations can be profit seeking (commercial companies) or not-for-profit (typically a charity) but they all need to be both governed and managed. And it the governance that is provided by the board.

This book – *Anticipating Disruption* - promotes what, to some, will be a controversial proposition: That the main role of a company board is to make predictions for the future of their organization and cause the organization to allocate resources and make plans accordingly. Governance, compliance, reporting and performance monitoring are essential basic tasks but charting a course for the future is the most important responsibility.

In recent years many boards have become obsessed with the issues of ESG – Environmental, Social and Governance. This fixation reflects the concerns of a wider society – at least in the Western world - where the challenges of climate change and the increased awareness of the need for gender and racial equality have reminded organizations that they do not function in a vacuum. It is now widely recognised and accepted that companies do have significant wider responsibilities. They are not just profit machines. They need to take environmental and social problems seriously. But in doing this they must not lose sight of the prime directive which is to ensure their organization thrives. And making the right call about the future is the main determinate of continuing to do well.

Boards provide "governance" which has its origins in the Greek verb "to steer". Directors provide direction, make decisions, allocate resources. Company law in the UK (section 172 of the 2006 Companies Act) says directors have a duty to "promote the success of the company" . The Act does not fully explain what "success" looks like but does go on to say directors (i.e. the members of the board) are seeking success "for the benefit of its Members as a whole" . Members in this context being shareholders. The Act goes on to say that this success seeking has to take account of the interests of others including, staff, suppliers and customers. The so-called "stakeholders". Current social norms and company law make the job of a board a complex balancing act.

Maximising Shareholder Value

When I was at the consulting firm McKinsey in the 1980s a recently published book was regarded as a near religious text when it came to defining what a company (and its board) was for. *Creating Shareholder Value* by Alfred Rappaport provided a single metric for judging corporate success – did the activity of the company create economic value for its shareholders. All other aspects of performance were said to be of secondary importance. It was an intellectual framework built on the practical management ideas of CEOs like Jack Welch of General Electric and before him the theoretical work of Nobel prize winning economist Milton Friedman.

Freidman laid out his ideas in an essay in the *New York Times* magazine in September 1970 entitled. "The Social Responsibility of Business is to Increase its Profits" In simple terms he argued that if a board allocated resources to goals other than making profit such as charitable donations, social or environmental objectives they were failing in their duty to shareholders. The argument was that the company should make the shareholders richer and they – the shareholders - could then spend their profits as they saw fit. The Friedman doctrine of the 1970s, as expressed by Rappaport and others in the 1980s, was seductively simple. When taken to the extreme it meant that all decisions such as reducing headcount, acquisitions, building new factories and capital allocations would be based on a simple, single idea – make more money for shareholders.

Since the Global Financial Crisis in 2007 and with 30 years of social and political developments related to climate change, consumer protection and minority rights this notion of shareholder value as the sole guiding principle would be regarded by most people today as overly simplistic or indeed dangerous. We now talk much more about creating *stakeholder* value recognising that the shareholders are just one constituency with a legitimate interest in the actions of a company.

Boards must now take a rounded stakeholder perspective not just a narrow shareholder perspective However given that this normally means developing a good relationship with customers, suppliers, staff, regulators, politicians and campaigners this is usually the right thing in terms of creating long-term shareholder value. Meeting ESG expectations should not be seen as a tiresome obligation but asced the best way of ensuring a bright future by being in tune with the developing norms of society. Being a social pariah is hardly the right position for a company wishing to thrive.

The Board Balancing Act

As the demands of ESG and challenges of broad stakeholder management have come to the fore it demands a complex balancing act from directors. How do you assess and react to the, inevitably, competing demands? Customers want lower prices which will often conflict with paying higher wages. More environmentally friendly manufacturing processes will win praise but may result in more expensive products.

Some of the stakeholder requirements are non-negotiable such as laws and regulations and the board needs to keep up to date and ensure compliance. Others such as energy consumption, treatment of suppliers, complaint handling, positive discrimination to drive diversity are matters of judgement. Boards do not have to prioritise these goals but there will be a downside in not doing so.

This book argues that the main role of a board is to be the forum where the future of an organization is discussed and that implies rather that simply reacting to evolving ESG requirements board needs to anticipate and get ahead of them. The non-profit objectives for companies will only grow. Responsible employers have tried to ensure that all parts of their supply chain treated their workers properly but that moved from being a laudable corporate policy to becoming a legal requirement with the Modern Slavery Act in 2015.

Getting the balancing act right means anticipating where ESG is going. This will vary by organization but as a broad observation tougher laws and regulations are coming on the use of energy (carbon taxes), all forms of pollution (externalities), data privacy, sick pay, shared parental leave, workplace safety and consumer protection. A regressive board will lobby to hold up new regulation. A progressive bard will have seen it coming and already modified their business processes to comply.

Stakeholder Surrogates

One way of approaching the balancing act is to try to ensure that the views of all stakeholders are represented at the board. But given the wide range of such stakeholders this is an impossible challenge. To have them all "present" at the board table, in the sense of being physically represented, is impractical. Directors are required to make decisions on behalf of stakeholders and boards are not intended to be structured as representative democracies.

Organizations must keep a lot of people happy. Employees, customers, regulators, suppliers, media commentators. It can be hard for full-time executives, focused on the day job, to "stand in the shoes" of all these stakeholders and make the balancing judgements of conflicting desires. Quite rightly the executives tend to see their organization through the lens of delivering operational excellence. But with a diverse group of non-executives added to the executives the board, as a whole, can play a valuable role in acting as a surrogate for multiple stakeholders by considering a range of external views.

It is extraordinary, in retrospect, that the mining company Rio Tinto decided it was "OK" to dynamite a 46,000 year old Aboriginal cave complex in Western Australia which had been declared a site of great archaeological and religious significance.[2] Surely had the board discussed it with an eye to the future rather than a short term operational benefit they would have said "hold on" which would have saved the CEO from being fired and the company suffering huge reputational damage. All it would have taken was one board member to place themselves in the mind-set of the conservationists , politicians and institutional investors.

The board needs to have a clear view of who its stakeholders are and ensure they are taken into consideration. This requires directors to be aware of external opinion and, when they feel it appropriate, champion the cause of stakeholders who are not present at the table. It can be one of the most valuable of roles of the NEDs to let executive see how a decision may play out when it reaches the wider public.

Board Composition

A company board is not intended to be a representative parliament of all elements of society or senate made up of geographically selected members. It is a group, which is essentially self-selected, but approved by a shareholder vote. It is there to provide governance, monitoring and to devise a strategy. To be effective it does need to understand and respond to the wide stakeholder group and to be cognisant of stakeholder needs and opinions. However it is not required to have appointed representatives of each stakeholder group so directors, particular nonexecutive directors, need to "stand in the shoes" of all stakeholders and listen to their views.

---

[2] The Age 20 December 2022 https://www.theage.com.au

In smaller, private companies with a few shareholders – a typical private equity structure – the shareholders often appoint a direct representative – an investor director - to protect their specific interests. In large public company investment institutions get to vote on the appointment of directors but vary rarely install their own person. Apart from the administrative challenge of finding large numbers of representatives when you own stakes in dozens of companies having a board seat deems an investor to be an "insider" (i.e. in receipt of inside privileged information). In listed companies this restricts their ability to trade in shares which most institutions would regard as unacceptable. Institutions find this lack of flexibility a problem and are happy to allow independent non-executives to look after their interests.

Executive directors are in place on a board because, presumably, they are good at their job and being directors is part of their employment contract. But the criteria for appointing non-executive appointments are far less clear cut. Typically boards will try to have a range of skills and backgrounds to provide a counterpoint to the specialist executives.

Some countries have laws which require workers representatives on boards. This present challenges of who selects those representatives - workplace ballot, trade unions, chosen by the board? In most cases countries which require employee board members have a two tier board structure with a rather remote supervisory board which includes the worker representatives and which discusses high level policy issues and a management board which actually runs the place

Many countries and regulatory authorities have guidelines seeking to appoint more women directors and a small but increasing number seek more directors with a BAME (Black, Asian and Minority Ethnic) background. Having a mix of gender and ethnicity often helps a board to understand broad stakeholders concerns but it is impractical and rather demeaning to suggest that women or BAME directors in some way sit as representative of their sex or race. All directors , irrespective of background, have the same legal responsibility to act in ways to promote the company itself. They are not there to argue the case for any special interest group.

To provide their oversight function some of the independent directors do need to have expertise in specific areas. Typical one NED is an ex accountant with the technical skills to be the Chair of the Audit Committee. And another will have the specialist knowledge of payment practices to chair Remuneration. Boards also tend to look for past experience specific to the needs of the company   This might be in a technology or a discipline such as marketing or perhaps a person with knowledge of a major target market or someone who understands the mindset of regulators and politicians.

Another reason boards would find it hard to have representative directors is size. It is generally accepted that there should be a majority of independent nonexecutives. So if a company has three executive members that suggests at least 4 NEDs giving seven. Anyone who has chaired a board knows that once you have more than about 9 people around a table it becomes exponentially more difficult to have a functional and satisfactory meeting. It becomes very hard to allow all members to participate in discussions. Old fashioned, large traditional companies tend to have large boards in the mistaken belief it makes them stronger and more representative. Normally it just provides an opportunity for people to get in each other's way. Boards which are too big tend to be overly formal and loose agility -they tend to become more regressive than progressive just as a result of size.

Diversity of Thought

If boards are to be successful in predicting the future for their organization, they must avoid linear group-think and have a wide variety of skills and backgrounds at the table. Diversity of background, experience and thought processes are what seems to mark out superior corporate performance. The diversity occasioned by having female and BAME directors helps but does not address fully the need to have a range of views.

For many years boardrooms were dominated by men. Women directors were rare largely because women executives were rare. Political and social pressure has changed this. Far more women are choosing to pursue executive careers so far more experienced women became available as valued NEDs. It would be very rare now to find an all-male board. And the evidence suggests a good gender balance does produce good financial results. This must make sense as broadly half of a company's customers, staff and suppliers are likely to be female.

Where diversity is more challenge and politically charged is in respect of minority communities. Disabled, gay, BAME individuals who might suffer discrimination at times. How does a board reflect their legitimate interests? An old Etonian with a degree from Oxford and an MBA from Harvard may be from a BAME background but is hardly a typical representative of the BAME community any more than they are a typical representative of any broad society. Its an extreme example but illustrates the point. In countries like Canada where many generations of BAME families have thrived and achieved the highest levels in education and in business there is a widespread BAME representation without the need for legislation or rules.

It would be relatively easy to construct board of NEDs including a large proportion of female and BAME individuals all of whom are privately educated, Oxbridge graduates who have worked in an investment bank and are now in their 50s. There are quite a few like this around. They would look suitably and balanced in the board photograph but their perspectives on business and society are likely to be highly monocultural.

I find myself in agreement with Dame Sharon White the (black British, highly qualified, highly successful) Chairman of John Lewis and ex CEO of Ofcom who does not regard BAME as a meaningful term as it encompasses such very diverse backgrounds. [3] Nonexecutives should certainly be cognisant of the challenges facing minority groups and support decisions to provide more equality, but to try to have all such groups represented in director roles is impossible. Diversity of thought and experience is the ideal outcome which does not always follow from selection process based on quotas.

Pareidolia is the human tendency to want to make sense of things by seeing patterns which are not really there. The much quoted example is the face of the "man in the moon" but it's the same effect with seeing a smile in the structure of the front of a car (headlights and radiator) or images of animals in cloud formations. Our brains impute patterns to attempt to extract the signal from the noise. A monocultural board made up of executives and ex-executives from the same industry all with similar backgrounds will tend to interpret information using the lens of the *status quo* and finding patterns which support the consensus industry view. A diverse board is more likely to look deeper at the same data for potentially surprising or unexpected meanings about what the future might bring.

---

[3] Sunday Times 23rd August 2020

The Role of Executive Directors

A company's management team is often called "the C suite" as in the CEO, CFO, CMO etc. or typically in Silicon Valley - "the ELT" the Executive Leadership Team. These are the men and women who run the organization on a day-to-day basis. They are full-time managers focused on solving immediate problems and executing "BaU" - Business as Usual.

A danger for the C-Suite or ELT is, as a group, is they can easily fall into the linear thinking of A leads to B lead to C. "10% growth in quarterly profits is twice as good as 5%". "We must hit this year's earnings target." This is not a criticism of executive management teams. It's an observation of real behaviour. This mindset is an inevitable outcome of the task at hand. I was part of a C-Suite for some 20 years, the last 10 of which I was a CEO. Looking back I know how necessary it was to manage the here and now rather than worry too much about the future. I found the focus on short-term task-orientation very attractive in my executive role.

But some of the C Suite individuals will also be members of the board. Typically just the CEO and CFO but sometimes others as well. It is in their board role they have the opportunity, indeed the obligation, to look around corners, anticipate and think long term.

The board is the place where executive skills and operating knowledge combine with non-executive experience and perspective. This group of directors needs to be able to agree upon and articulate three main ideas: Purpose, vision and narrative. Purpose is why the organization exists -what is it for. Vision is what the organization hopes to be and how it plans to achieve its goals. Narrative is the organizations story - the way it presents itself to stakeholders.

Each board develops its own unique style, cadence, and processes. Each is made up of a different grouping of individuals dealing with different issues and industries. At first sight one board meeting might look much like another but dig deeper and each has its own idiosyncrasies. However, there are three broad types of behaviours boards should try to avoid but which seem all too common. They are the board acting as an inquisition, as a management committee and as a debating society. These extremes of behaviour type do not help the organization progress.

Inquisitional boards see themselves as a sort of distanced, supervisory controlling elite. They feel they need to act as regulators or corporate police. Budget and bonus goals are set higher than the management recommends to "put them under pressure". Executives are scolded for missing targets. It is an "us and them" approach. NEDs pride themselves on being "tough" by subjecting the executives to interrogation. Executives become tempted to report only the good news. Boards like this are a dysfunctional nightmare of two warring tribes, mistrust and political intrigue. This approach can happen with private equity owners who develop a belief that only by their intervention will management reach peak performance. It can also happen in not-for-profits where a board of the "great and good" develop unrealistic expectations of managers working with limited resources.

The board as *management committee* approach is where all directors gets immersed in detail and lose sight of the big picture. Lengthy conversations go into the micromanagement of operational units or the specifics of particular customers. NEDs start acting like executives and often revert to their own past executive careers. Phrases like "in my own (by implication extensive and relevant) experience…" and "when we did this a Company X…." should ring alarm bells.

Management committee boards spend their time looking backwards. Directors want to agonize over monthly management reports, variance month on month, variance to prior year, variance to budget. It is reasonable and sensible for boards to note any big or unexpected shift in performance but going into fine detail simply replicates what the weekly or monthly management meeting already covers. It duplicates what the executive are already doing as their day-job and it wastes time. This is the "lost in the weeds" and "cannot see the woods for the trees" approach. These type of boards are using a magnifying glass when they should be reaching for a telescope.

The *debating club* board is typical of organizations which have enjoyed long-term success with a relatively unchanged business model and can indulge themselves by allowing board meetings to become the equivalent of a university discussion group. Non-executives directors are often well read and curious about the world. Some people like an audience. A board can be an ideal opportunity for delivering a lecture. It is an enjoyable temptation to use board time to discuss macro-economic issues like long-term interest rates, American politics or the price of gold. Such sessions are intellectually interesting but of very limited value in charting the course for the organization. Regurgitated articles from *The Economist* or *Harvard Business Review* make for a pleasing debate but led to an unproductive and probably pointless discussion. Of course, if your company is in the gold extraction or jewellery business the gold price is a legitimate board topic – but for most it is not.

Good boards are a team with a common goal who think about future organizational performance. They do supervise but they also speculate. They govern but also anticipate. Experienced and diverse NEDs work alongside knowledgeable executives to ask themselves questions about what might happen next. All board members bring to the table their past work and current contacts and knowledge but do not rely solely on their experiences to develop a blueprint for the future. They concern themselves with what is best for the organisation rather than seeking to assign blame for missed targets or seeking self-advancement in their own careers. The best boards are served by curated data and characterised by short, carefully edited board papers. Presentations describe the options and make clear recommendations rather than drowning directors in information.

When trying to form picture of future events boards receive multiple streams of information. Getting a clear understanding of the "signal", when it is obscured by a the huge volume of "noise" is no easy task. The board is the mechanism for trying to extract signal from noise and diverse boards are much better equipped to do this.

Progressive and Regressive Boards

In the "What Went Wrong" section I described the different responses to the arrival of the internet by the boards of the two UK-based publishing companies I chaired in the early 2000s. The long-established and very successful Johnston Press tended to look backwards and reacted to the new technology by doing more of the same. The much younger and less corporately self-assured Future board looked (living up to its name) towards what they thought would happen next in the media industry. It is worth noting that Johnston had the near unanimous and vocal support of its shareholders for its conservative approach. Future had a small number of equally vocal institutional critics who were unconvinced by it wanting to innovate and demanded short term earnings and dividends.

In the sections that follow in the "What If…? chapter I am using the idea that boards fall into two extreme states of mind. Two opposite ends of the spectrum. Progressive and Regressive boards. This characterisation is obviously a gross over-simplification. No group of people would come together to create such extreme board behaviours but the exaggeration of the end points of a spectrum is a useful device.

Progressive boards take the view that most aspects of their environment will change and accept they may have to sacrifice short term cash profits for investment in resources and skills to prepare for those changes. They see the future as an opportunity.

Regressive boards take the view that past success confirms their business model and approach are correct and assume that they will continue to do well by sticking to their guns and investing to support their current ways of working. They assume the future looks like the past and feel "If it ain't broke – don't fix it'

To provide an hypothetical example from the publishing industry how does the board react in the face of criticism that printing on paper is bad for the environment. The regressive board seeks to comply with reporting requirements on paper use and responds (sometimes reluctantly and after lobbing for the *status quo*) to implement new regulations and legislation. The progressive board will seek ways to invest in the paper recycling business and look to accelerate digital distribution of content.

The list below are obviously extreme stereotypes of board attitudes. The vast majority of organizations will be a mixture of the two.

The Progressive Board

- Seeks information about industry trends.
- Curious and knowledgeable about competitors.
- Open to external ideas from consultants.
- Seeks to bring in outsiders as directors with new skills and experience.
- Knows what it does not know and seeks to learn.
- Anticipates regulations, seeks to align business processes in advance.
- Regards ESG developments as inevitable
- Embraces notion of stakeholder capitalism
- Asks "What If…?

The Regressive Board

- Focused on analysis of past financial results.
- Regards competitors as incompetent.
- Prefers internal analysis to external input.
- Values specific industry experience and being "one of us" in new directors
- Certain that its people are "the best in the industry"
- Complies with regulations but lobbies for their relaxation.
- Regards ESG as a nuisance.
- Leans to the shareholder value model
- Asks "Why…?

ASKING WHAT IF...?

The most effective boards envision their organization's future and interpret their task as going beyond monitoring management, reporting and maintaining a risk register of threats. They look at the potential opportunities thrown up by the evolution of technology, demographics, the environment, social attitudes and legislation. A careful analysis of current performance – asking why is there a variance to last year and why are we missing/meeting/beating budget is only part of the board's task. The real challenge is anticipating what might happen. Asking: What if...?

This book argues the true measure of the success of a board is the performance of the organization over a long time - the ability to be agile and navigate the future. And in this context the most important role of the board is to see around corners – to prepare for what might happen next. To anticipate discontinuities and disruption and look at ways to benefit. But this does nor mean the board should seek to become economic or social forecasters. Expert predictions are widely available from investment banks, think tanks and consultants. A board simply needs to have a consensus on which forecasts they choose to adopt. They can then build their strategy upon an agreed vison of the future.

The meetings of the board provide the forum for the executives and non-executives to combine their skills, experience and ideas to rise above basic performance monitoring and unite in asking themselves how do we position our organization to thrive in new circumstances. The executives are at these meetings in their capacity as directors – they bring to the table their operational knowledge of the company but they, along with the non-executive colleagues, as directors have the task of planning long term actions.

This next section of the book assumes a board is already doing all the normal hygiene tasks: scrutinising management accounts, ensuring regulatory compliance, approving numbers for reporting, controlling remuneration etc. The board, almost certainly, will have a risk management process which can vary from the most cursory box ticking to lengthy debates about various scenarios and mitigating actions. But having done all this some of the board's time should be devoted to the "what happens next and what are our options?" questions. Ideally this discussion forms part of every meeting and is not just done once a year at the strategy away-day.

Anticipation goes beyond analysing trends. Trends are linear projections. Anticipation considers the unexpected. Budgeting (a 12 month time horizon) and planning (typically looking three years ahead) are normally based on an extrapolation of recently observed data. Sales, margins, areas of growth, areas of decline etc. This is useful – as far as it goes. Ideally anticipation includes looking for potential discontinuities, inflection points, and discussing their impact. A new tax regime, new government, new competitors or a new technology. Major changes in consumer sentiment, a war , a natural disaster, a pandemic. The "what-if" questions. These considerations includes potential upside as well as downsides – unlike the now ubiquitous Risk Register which is usually a gloomy list of potential pitfalls with obvious, but not necessarily effective, mitigations.

Risk Register Rituals

Keeping a risk register has become a regulatory requirement for some listed companies and most other boards public, private and not-for-profit, have now adopted the approach. The idea is a formal process to identify things that might be a problem and then to categorise them into how likely to happen and how much of an impact they would have on the organization. Then to describe actions to mitigate the effects. Typically risk registers are full of theoretical events - bad happenings such as a fire, flood, failure of IT system, resignations or illness of key staff. The likelihood and impact of each is assessed often using the "RAG" - Red Amber Green - traffic light approach.

To take an extreme case a powerful earthquake in London would be regarded as being a very high impact event (Red) but one with a low likelihood of happening (Green) . The mitigation is likely to include having a back-up data centre in a remote location.

More typical is "Senior member of Executive team is taken seriously ill" - high impact (Red) with a medium risk of happening (Amber). The mitigation will be to have detailed succession plans in place.

In one sense the Risk Register does exactly what this book calls for – it is a device to force boards to think about the future. But it tends to focus on being ready for obvious negative events and not thinking about how to position the organization to thrive in the face of change. It can also result in an illusion of control and becomes an annual ceremony which gives the impression of thinking about the future but actually becomes a ritualistic box ticking exercise – in the most extreme cases answers are cut and pasted from another company's annual report. The creation of the RAG charts becomes an end in itself and precludes a genuine debate about what might happen next.

Maintaining the Risk Register is potentially useful, and in some cases a requirement, but it should not get in the way of a board being curious. about a wide range of possibilities.

Being Curious

Boards spend lots of time, in some cases too much time, looking at metrics which describe the past. Sales, operating margins, cash flow are all retrospective information. These numbers offer what seems to be unambiguous data which can be compared with past months, quarters and years. Trends can be identified. Variances interrogated. Directors usually like this type of "hard" data as they are not being asked to confront hypothetical situations. It is a comfort zone for those with a background in accountancy and auditing. It is the rear-view mirror style of corporate driving.

As described above boards also look at the mitigation of downside problems in the risk register process but this does not invite open discussion of opportunities. To navigate successfully the future boards need to seek out leading indicators and consider data which is messy and full of conjecture and "noise". Predictions about changes in customer behaviour, speculation about new legislation and forecasts about the use of technology. But this is what effective board must do – look ahead through the windscreen.

Tell even the most dyed-in-the wool regressive board about the driving analogy and they will insist they understand that the road ahead is far more important than the road behind. They will endorse the windscreen view, in theory, but will still try to build strategy on the foundations of the events of the past. For these boards the budgeting and planning processes are far more an extrapolation of the management accounts than they are an open-minded forecast of market potential.

SONAR, RADAR, and LIDAR. The "..DAR" stands for "Detection and Ranging" using Sound, Radio, and Light in each case. Finding an object using the reflection of different types of waves and then working out how far away it is has widespread military and civilian uses. Companies also need Detection and Ranging systems but this requires a corporate version of sending out sound, radio and light waves. Boards need to take active steps to make enquiries, generate information and then separate the signal from the noise.

Organizations are not trying to locate objects in a three dimensional space – the function of the various DAR's - they are seeking to understand how aspects of their environment will change. They have to do this by asking questions and identifying trends by monitoring the changes in behaviour of their customers, competitors suppliers and regulators and taking a view about what these developments in technology and social attitudes will mean for their organization. There can be no certainties about future conditions but boards need to form a collective view and then act upon it.

A challenge with all the Detection and Ranging technologies is the distinction between signal and noise. When the target is a long way off the receptors will pick up a lot of noise – false reflections. By the time the signal is perfectly strong the target is probably too close to take appropriate action. The same challenge faces a corporation when it is seeking a sense of direction. Vast amounts of information flood in. Numerous, often contradictory, consultants reports, market research projects, customer surveys and white papers about potential government policy.

Boards need to decide at what point evidence of behaviour indicates what may become a significant shift in customer demands. In the year 2000 about 5% of the UK population declared they were vegetarian. By 2020 this had nearly doubled to just under 10% but amongst Millennials (born 1981 to 1996) the proportion is higher at 15%. Back in 2000 the trend away from eating animal products would have been a weak signal from high-end Californian grocery stores. But now catering to vegetarian consumers is a mainstream, big business. Organizations which got this right have enjoyed a significant advantage. It is a similar story with ecommerce, mobile phones and electric vehicles- the trends were there to be seen bot not all businesses acted upon them.

Organizations often commission large amounts of market research. Surveys, focus groups, product tests (and as the Chairman of a leading market research company – YouGov – I am very grateful for this) but to a great extent this approach is predicated but defining what sort of insights you are looking for. Structured consulting projects based on specific market surveys are not always the best way to highlight unexpected discontinuities. That needs creative thinking informed by weak signals.

To get a good feel for likely changes coming the people best placed to pick up the strongest signals are executives working at the front line in sales, customer relations, procurement and HR. The finance function who provide the bulk of the board's information are, by design, looking at the past. The board which wants to be curious needs to ensure it is listening to people who are the closest to future trends.

False Assumptions

Most companies and their boards operate with a common set of assumptions about how their organization works and what the future holds. They arrive at these accepted "truths" because they are what their company and its directors have experienced and which, in some cases, are the beliefs that underpin their companies reason for being. Some internally accepted corporate "truths" are safe bets – "people will still need to eat". Other less certain – "people will still need to buy food in shops". Others very debatable – "people will always buy newspapers". But boards and managers are still making decisions based on these type of settled and accepted assumptions.

Those running big grocery stores are aware of the shift to online shopping and the growth of take-away food, but many traditional managers assume this would impact their in-store sales only by a few percent at the margin and not threaten their existence. They might be in for a nasty shock.

In 2006 I was part of a private equity team at Permira seeking to acquire the HMV music and video chain. We took the view that the distribution of entertainment was going digital and HMV needed to reduce radically the number of stores it owned from 350 to below 100 and invest in digital. We offered some £900 million for the "privilege" of taking over and fixing the problem. The board, who has access to the same data as us, rejected the offer out of hand and were supported by traditional shareholders. They stuck to their guns. HMV went bust in 2013.

As chairman of a local newspaper company in the 2000s I was told with great confidence at boards meetings that the arrival of the internet might depress advertising by "a few percentage points" and our plans should be based on that. It actually dropped more than 20% in 2 years. Newspaper publishers are still approving expensive equipment purchases and making hiring decisions based on the assumption that the printed newspaper format will be around for a long-time. They need a Plan B in case they are wrong. Many industry observers think print is doomed which is why pessimistic investors take short positions in newspaper shares but some boards continue to believe the past is a good guide to the future and continue to support the old model.

Hindsight, of course, makes it very easy to see past mistakes but even so it is interesting to see how errors in assumptions came about. Listed below are some of the conversations that I recall from my days as chairman of a local newspaper business in the 2000s.

"If advertisers want to reach local people they have to use the local paper."

The fact that websites are designed for, and accessible by, a global audience tended to blind newspaper managers to the reality that they could also be positioned to serve a hyper local audience. A web site viewer wanting to catch up on celebrity gossip does not care where the content is created but the business advertiser is able to target and pay for just those that live in a selected local area. National, indeed global, content attracts the multiple local audiences which are then sold to those who value them most. Once local advertisers had worked this out the viability of the local newspaper model was hopelessly compromised. It seems obvious now but in the 2000s many newspaper mangers refused to see this coming.

"People really value local news"

This is broadly true. News about tree that's fallen at the end of your road will be more interesting and relevant to you than news about an earthquake on the other side of the world. However, newspaper boards had available to them lots of research that demonstrated that much of the motivation for reading a local newspaper was, in fact, to access the local advertising that the reader felt relevant to them. People looking to buy a car would read the motoring pages, those thinking of buying a selling and a house wanted to test out the property market and those considering a move of job or who were currently not working wanted to see the employment ads.

Once these types of advertising listings could be made available online, which they were in huge numbers in the 2000s, and once they could be searched using simple tools it should have been fairly obviously one of the main motivations for reading a local newspaper – the local advertising - would fall away.

The error in the board assumption was to assume that local "news", in the mind of the reader, was the activities of local council and local crime when, in fact, many readers saw the advertising as the most important "news" as it told them about what homes and car could be purchased locally and for how much.

"Local newspapers were not badly hit by the arrival of television. They'll survive the internet"

This was broadly true of television and indeed radio but of course was not an appropriate analogy. Television is a regional and national medium. TV coverage of local activity at a town level was very limited. And TV advertising was too expensive for local estate agents and car dealers. But the internet and web sites presented a very different threat as they could be based upon local advertising and had no obligation to take on the cost of reporting local news.

Also the development of commercial television in the UK happened at a time of economic boom which masked the relative decline of newspapers. Surviving the arrival of television in the 1960s did not imply immunity from the internet in the 2000s

"Buying the local paper is a deeply ingrained habit"

This was true of those aged over 60 who regarded a newspaper purchase as part of their normal visit to the corner store, supermarket or newsagents. But younger people increasingly engaged with, and were informed about, their local communities via social media. As the smoking habit dramatically reduced and take-away food grew in popularity the trip to the corner store was less frequent. And when the UK introduced a national lottery evidence suggests than some older consumers switched their newsagent habit by buying a lottery ticket rather than a paper. I very much doubt many newspaper boardrooms predicted the impact the national lottery would have.

The examples above are all from a local newspaper business but the same principle applies to any boardroom. Directors have a habit of making assumptions which support the continued existence of their conventional business model. Boards need to be more open minded. And, crucially, cannot assume the past is a guide to the future. A board needs to articulate and then challenge the "truths" which they believe underpin their existence. They also need to really understand their own business model – its strengths and weaknesses.

Understand your own economics

A vital task for the board is to ensure they a have a common view of the true economics of their own business. Anticipating the future can only be effective if the real sources of value added, the problem being solved for customers, the reasons for making a profit – are correctly identified and understood.

Executives in specific areas of the organization will often see the economics of the business through the lens of their own speciality. Sales will, unsurprisingly and correctly, focus on revenues, the finance team may look at cost allocation, production will strive for efficiency, HR will be seeking improved productivity and reduced recruitment cost. But the board needs to have an holistic overview and understand why their organization exists and why its customers really value it.

If you had asked the board directors of local newspaper companies in the 1990s and even 2000s what was the value created by their businesses most would have said it was the provision of accurate and timely local news which caused people to want to buy the paper and that created the audience which allowed them to sell advertising . As noted in the section above the truth was that readers really valued accessing the advertising and the information it gave them about cars, houses and jobs. They liked the news coverage as a sort of bonus. Once cheaper (in fact free) alternatives came along on the web the prevailing beliefs about local newspaper economics were demonstrably refuted.

It was certainly true, from my own experience at Johnston Press, that the board's view was they were in the local news business.

That was why the internet caused so much damage as directors were looking in the wrong direction .

At the magazine company Future, at first sight, the company's main source of value added seemed to be publishing specialist titles which informed and entertained people in the rapidly growing industry of computer gaming. But the board looked beyond this and realised a lot of customers purchased the magazine to obtain a DVD that was affixed to the cover which contained additional characters or game levels or "cheats" for their favourite game. The magazine, to the reader was mainly a distribution mechanism for the digital content on the discs – the magazine content was a bonus. Advised by the management the board took the view that the internet would, in time, wholly replace this physical disc as a channel to obtain game enhancements and whilst it would not directly impact the magazine it would fundamentally undermine the economics. Future invested in digital distribution of content in the belief their current (highly profitable) model would disappear quite quickly. It did but the business was ready.

Future also realised that many if its readers used the magazines to help them make purchase decisions - cameras, PCs, electronics, bicycles, games, films and more. This led to the realisation that the web sites should be far more focused on product reviews than other sort of content and that in time the web sites should have direct links to retailers. This is now the common and accepted e-commerce model but at the time was radical and not endorsed by traditional journalists or shareholders.

In considering their economics and trying to impress investors commercial organizations typically talk a great deal about sales and profits and will stress the value of the assets that they own. But to correctly anticipate what is coming next the board must consider intangibles and externalities which are not always visible on financial statements.

In the 2000s many traditional retailers scoffed at Amazon arguing that because it appeared to be loss making and had limited physical assets its multi billion dollar valuation was false. But of course Amazon had relationships with, knew about the buying habits of, and held the email address and credit card details for many tens of millions of happy customers. This intangible value was "seen" by some enlightened investors but apparently not visible to conventional competitors. Traditional retailers who often did not know their customers names or addresses – let alone their buying habits - reassured themselves that Amazon would run out of money. This failed to anticipate that Amazon would, one day, cash-in on that hugely valuable intangible asset of a customer relationship.

Oil companies, car makers and airlines all have significant externalities – in that they create pollution which is a cost to society but does not directly appear as a cost to them in their P&L. As with positive intangibles investors sense this and the share prices reflect these concerns. The boards of these companies also recognise the challenges of the externalities but maybe underestimate the problems to come given the huge head of steam (probably a bad metaphor in this context) built up by environmental campaigners who are clearly moving from the fringe to be at the centre of political activity.

One of the drivers of an organization's economics and its profitability is the relative strength of the forces acting upon it. The most obvious is the activity of existing competitors but also the relative negotiating power of suppliers and customers; the availability of substitutes and the ease of entry by new competitors.

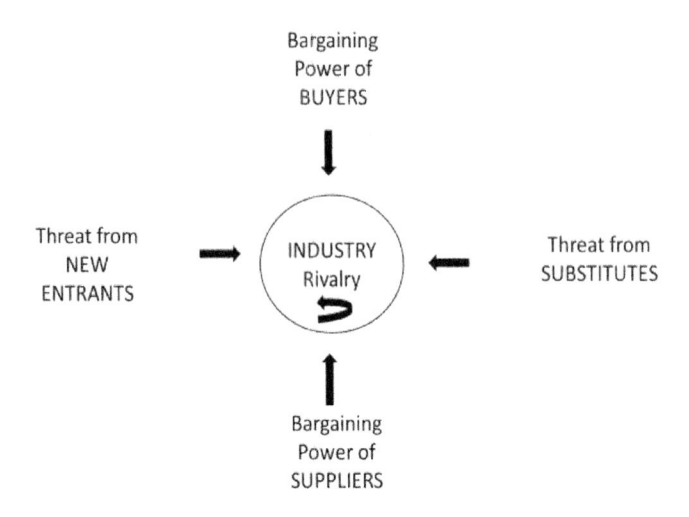

```
                    Bargaining
                    Power of
                    BUYERS
                       │
                       ▼
   Threat from      ┌─────────┐      Threat from
      NEW       ──▶ │ INDUSTRY │ ◀── SUBSTITUTES
   ENTRANTS        │  Rivalry  │
                    └─────────┘
                       ▲
                       │
                    Bargaining
                    Power of
                    SUPPLIERS
```

This is the famous "five forces" model of Harvard professor Michael Porter which provides a way to analyse the likely of the level of competition in an industry. The logic being that if all five forces are weak the industry will be very profitable but as one or more of the forces becomes strong profitability declines.

British supermarkets, for example, have much more market power than most of their suppliers (supermarkets are bigger than farmers) and more than their buyers (i.e. individual consumers who are purchasing small amounts and are unable to negotiate bulk discounts). There are no substitutes for food and small local food shops cannot compete on range and price. Barriers to entry are relatively high although the discounters Aldi and Lidl and online grocers like Ocado have found a way in. But for many years it was only intense rivalry between the big four have kept their profits relatively low.

The five forces model is useful at an industry level. It provides less insight when applied to an individual firm but none the less is a good starting point for a board wanting to ask questions about what the future might look like.

A particular challenge which has emerged in the decades since the Porter model was conceived is the role of the tech. giants. Apple, Alibaba , Alphabet (Google) Amazon and their like can potentially disrupt almost any industry. Did camera makers expect to be eclipsed by the iPhone? Did taxis (and car makers) expect the disruption of Uber. Did British supermarkets predict the impact of Just Eat ? Almost every established industry now potentially competes with a tech giant.

The rest of this section suggests way in which boards should push themselves to ask the What If…? questions and then discuss how their organization can be prepared in some of the What Ifs happen.

Competitors

Executives tend to view relations with competitors in terms of a zero-sum game – I certainly did when I was a CEO. "A sale lost to Competitor X is a transfer of value away from us".   Competitors do things that annoy you. They may cut prices, target your best customers, launch "me-too" products, poach your best staff, offer better deals to your supplier. Managers, with the need to maintain morale, are prone to dismiss competitors as hopelessly inept or as unreasonably aggressive to the point of implying questionably illegal tactics. In many years as an executive myself this was sometimes our teams view. It is usually too narrow a perspective. Boards can lift their eyes from the day to day battle and be more balanced. Competitors behaviour can be a useful guide to the future.

Competitors probably have access to the same predictive information that you do but may interpret and act on it in different ways . They will have their own plans for new products, new markets and new technologies. To some extent this information will be available in company presentations, stock market analyst notes, press interviews and general market intelligence. Hiring competitors' staff can be a goldmine of legitimate information but don't ask them to bring their confidential files with them.

Competitor companies may come up for sale. It is advantageous to know as far in advance as possible if this is likely. It is always worth putting in a bid if a competitor's company is placed in an auction process. The information memorandum will be useful perspective on your market. An acquisition of a rival might represent an opportunity to acquire new customers and gain market share or if its done by a well-financed new owner they might be a bigger threat. Having good insight into the possibilities and having considered the What If …? of doing a deal should mean the business and its advisers are ready to move quickly. As with all other areas a board is not able to predict definitively the future but they can make well informed assumptions and plan accordingly.

Progressive boards will keep an updated and detailed file on competitors which can be regularly presented to directors. Information about movements in market share, pricing, discounting, promotions, advertising spend are all part of the monitoring of business-as-usual. For the long term the "What If..?" questions are more valuable. Is a change of top management likely because of age or internal strife. Are the competitor's shareholders happy? Is the ownership likely to change. Could the competitor become a target for acquisition by us or by someone else. Is the competitor gearing up to buy us These are very speculative but exactly the questions a curious board will be asking themselves.

The approach is not only to ask: Why did a competitor do that? But what if a competitor did this ?

Most companies will have extensive data on the behaviour of customers and potential customers. The marketing department can do multiple segmentations by age, location, income, habits and lifestyle. Analysis is available on demographics, psychographics, share of wallet etc. The Chief Marketing Officer can always be summoned to a meeting laden with PowerPoint charts and facts. Companies tend to know a reasonable amount about what their customers have been and are doing but do boards really ask themselves what will happen if something significant changes.

The executive team will always be looking for customer feedback to drive product improvements and launches. It is what good managers do. The role of the board is to try to prepare the organization for radical shifts in customer behaviour. This is difficult as customers rarely know themselves what they might do differently next year. They respond to events. It might be a health scare that puts people off eating eggs. A tax rise that makes car driving far more expensive. A new TV station that suddenly takes half the established audience away. The customer did not know any of these things were coming so would not have been able to predict they planned to change their habits.

Aside from unexpected events it is , in theory, possible to anticipate consumer trends using research. The problem with asking people is they don't really know until confronted with actual options. They can tell you with some certainty if they plan to but car in the next 12 months. And whether it will be petrol, hybrid or electric, family saloon or four door sports. They know the options, their specific requirements and know their budget. But in response to questions about hypotheticals whether they will switch allegiance from conventional yoghurt to Greek style its hard for a consumer to be accurate in predicting their own behaviour until the options are in front of them.

A company running stores aimed at new mothers is likely to know a lot about the attitudes and behaviours of the current generation of pregnant, and just delivered, women. But how much do they really know about what girls, currently at school, will be like when their turn comes. Will they have the same approach as their older sisters or will there be a dramatic discontinuity driven by technology or medical science in the way they handle having a new child in the house.

The challenge has been made harder by the arrival of social media and the rise of "influencers" who can cause dramatic changes in a very short time frame. And its not just 20 somethings on TicToc who can exhibit radical change. If David Attenborough comes out against plastic packaging or Mary Berry suggests a new recipe using ginger an immediate, and hard to have predicted, impact will be seen in peoples buying habits.

Boards should make the time to discuss what might happen to the behaviour of their own established customer group in the event of social changes and events. Do not just extrapolate. Be ready for disruption. Always be asking: "What will customers want next?"

Substitutes

Boards and executives normally know a lot about, and spend much time discussing, customers and competitors. The more opaque idea of potential substitute products or services is likely to get less board time. The threat of substitutes (or the ability for your product to become one) is commonly overlooked but as digital technology allows many business to converge on each other it deserves investigation. The questions include: To what degree can our customers meet their needs with something else? And what is the chance that this something else may come along? Substitutes are not a competitor's alternative product they something which is different but serves the same consumer need. Tea is a substitute for coffee but so are fruit juices. Using a taxi is a substitute for owning a car – Uber is a substitute for both.

In the 2000s magazine publishers and TV broadcasters started to realise that computer games were a substitute for reading and viewing. The market they were addressing was not so much for advertising or subscriptions but competition for customers leisure time. There are, as the cliché reminds us, only 24 hours in a day. All that gaming time had to come from a reduction in other leisure activities. Traditional media lost out to an activity they would never have considered a competitor in a strict economic sense.

An average human male needs to take in about 2,500 calories a day. This might be food they eat in a restaurant, ready meals from a supermarket or food they buy and cook at home. Supermarkets long ago recognised that takeaway restaurants might take some of their trade and responded by offering ready-to-eat meals on their shelves. But the customer still needed to come to the store. Tech. start-ups like Just Eat, Deliveroo or Uber Eats make the takeaway option so much simpler to choose and then the Covid-19 pandemic made going to restaurant or supermarkets a lot more difficult. The delivery guy on a bike became the substitute for going somewhere to get a meal. And those services are now starting to offer home delivery groceries – in effect bringing the chilled food aisle into your home.

Automobile makers have traditionally seen public transport as a substitute for having a car. Consumers in the Baby Boom and Gen X cohorts regarded a car as a near vital purchase. But Millennials and Gen Z show much less interest in car ownership. Ride sharing services like Uber and Lyft are now seen as direct substitutes for car ownership.

During the pandemic all providers of transport - buses, trains, taxis and planes saw revenue collapse as their passengers turned to Zoom and Microsoft Teams . The substitute was unlikely to have been mentioned at many transport board meetings before it happened whereas the founders of Zoom specifically saw business travel as a market to contest to find revenue.

Managers, in their managerial role, will tend to focus on direct competitors. In their board role the threat/opportunity of substitutes is a classic example of anticipation. The questions are: What If my customers can achieve the same outcome by finding a viable substitute ?

Suppliers

The UK clothing store Marks & Spencer used to be famous for the very positive way it worked with suppliers. It had a buy-British policy and sought long term relationships with local manufacturers. It took trouble to ensure suppliers were paid on time and treated with respect. It earned a formidable and positive reputation. Cost pressures in the 1990s caused it to abandoned these polices and its market share of clothing has decline significantly.

A more successful and more recently created rival to M&S is the clothing group Zara whose highly agile supply chain allows it to get fashionable goods into stores very rapidly. It has used its superior logistics as a source of competitive advantage

The huge disruption of Brexit has caused many businesses to reassess their supply arrangements in fear of tariffs and congested ports. What was previously left to management as an operational detail has became a board level issue – partly as a result of extensive government publicity.

The supply chain can be a strategic issue for many organizations. It is an obvious one for car makers where a model assembled in one country will have parts for several others. But now new economy businesses like Deilveroo and Uber need to be concerned about where drivers and delivery riders will come from in the future – will new legislation about employment status make it harder to find people who want to work as full time employees when they have enjoyed being self-employed subcontractors ?

Negative events in the supply chain are usually reflected in the risk register. Typically a supplier going bankrupt or a rise in oil prices are identified with suitable mitigation but often boards are not curious enough to probe for events which might fundamentally change the way their organization operates because of changes in those who supply it.

Always be asking "What can we do to improve our relationship with suppliers?" and "what might change"

New Entrants

At the time Michael Porter was writing in the analogue 1980s "New Entrants" usually meant a start-up of a company who entered your market by offering something very similar to your product or service. In effect a new competitor in the making. The power of this "force" being the existence, or the lack of, barriers to entry such as a license to operate (banking) or a huge capital investment need (chemical plant).

Now in digital 2020s almost all companies face the possibility of losing customers to a tech. business which offers to solve their consumer problem in a different way. Amazon is an alternative to almost any retailer but increasingly will offer pharmacy services, insurance, medical consultation, banking, travel and much, much more. The very existence of Google means no professional service provider like a lawyer, accountant or even doctors are insulated from competition coming for almost anywhere in the world.

When Proctor & Gamble acquired the Gillette razor business in 2005 I wonder of they thought that the most active competitor in a decade's time would be on-line companies offering razors delivered on a regular subscriptions basis. It's a good illustration of the value of the standard business school question that boards should ask themselves: "What business are we really in?". The customer is not buying a razor or even buying a blade, what they seek is an effective shave with a blade that is always sharp. A subscription service offers this with the razors, blades and even the shaving foam as part of the package that arrives in your mail box – the entire conventional retail chain is broken.

Some combination of the internet (Google etc), smartphones (Apple etc) and home deliveries (Amazon etc) means that almost any company can now face a new entrant who fulfils the fundamental customer need but may bypass the traditional channels of distribution and marketing

Boards need to ensure they are getting information about emerging and novel ideas not just be briefed in detail on existing competitors. I was first told about Craig's List in year 2000 – I wish as a newspaper chairman I had commissioned more research into it in during its early days as that might have changed the history of my local newspaper company.

Demographics

Boom, Bust and Echo is a highly influential Canadian book of the late 1990s[4] which, for many people, was an early introduction to the, now, very familiar generational idea of Baby Boomers, Gen X and Millennials. The book argues that "demographics explains 2/3rds of everything" which in many aspects of society is true. Absent dramatic changes in immigration and emigration we can predict the age and make up of UK society for decades to come. By the 2050s the UK population will be around 80 million – 20% up on today, and the number of people over 70 substantially greater than today. We will be a larger and older nation which has clear implications for housing, schools, hospitals and energy. But will also have clear implications for corporations trying to map their future.

Demographic projections are no secret. They are official government data and are available to all so, arguably, are not a source of competitive advantage. But some boards seem to wilfully ignore the obvious when making decisions. Boards sometimes dismiss long term projections with the pejorative term "futurology." Sceptical directors will cite Malthus (the economist who stated in 1798 that because of population growth humanity would starve to death but failed to predict industrial agriculture and fertilisers) but demographic analysis does not involve making unsubstantiated assumptions. Demographic projections are very reliable. It is how you quantify the impact on your organization that is very open to interpretation.

It is a simple fact that in 30 years time in the UK there will be a significantly more pensioners and fewer young people and working

---

[4] *Boom, Bust and Echo* David K. Foot with Daniel Stoffman, Macfarlane, Walter and Ross, Toronto, 1996.

age adults. This has obvious implications for the sort of products and services which will be needed by consumers and for the availability of young employees. This picture is clear to all companies and should lead into discussions about investment in automation and robotics.

Even if a board starts from the view that 30 years is too long a time horizon to worry abut or even if they believe the new population structure will have no impact on their company they should at least have the discussion to ensure they do not overlook this most concrete of element of mapping the future.

Environment

Storms are more severe, weather is more extreme, sea levels are rising, flooding and forest fires are more common. At the time of writing the world is in the grip of the Covid-19 pandemic made worse, in part, by bad food hygiene, overcrowding and inadequate medical facilities.

People are genuinely worried about environmental issues. Politicians are reacting. So, in one way or another, the world is going greener and more environmentally conscious. Pollution, carbon release, excessive food miles, business travel, global health are all under pressure and this will increase as the negative aspects of the elegantly called Anthropocene – the epoch of human impact on the planet – are widely accepted.

Governments are legislating – banning diesel cars and taxing carbon emissions. Organizations in the front line of this such as oil companies, airlines and car makers are taking steps. But it is hard to imagine that any organization will be immune from the reaction to climate change. For some it's a threat but for others opportunity.

Companies are now aware that they have to look beyond the immediate profit goal and take actions consistent with being a good corporate citizen. Boards must consider the externalities caused by their operations. Pollution, carbon footprint, water usage, packaging etc.

Boards will be discussing the obvious actions – consistent with he ESG obligations. Looking for low energy solutions, better insulation, less business travel. But are they looking at the second and third order effects of environmental change? Electric vehicle charging points will become as familiar as lamp posts. What does that imply for your organization. A drive to replace the nation's gas boilers will need tens of thousand more heating engineers. They will need recruitment and training.

This book references the newspaper and magazine industries. I find it very hard to believe that the huge, negative environmental impact of printing with ink on paper and then physically distributing the publication by road can possibly survive the pressures of climate concerns. In extreme cases some countries may make mass commercial printing on paper illegal, many will introduce less favourable taxation regimes and younger consumers are likely to boycott the printed medium on environmental grounds. And yet in boardrooms around the world investment continues to be made in the old printing technology.

The environmental opportunities and threats will vary between types of company but the significant changes in public attitudes and legislative response mean that no board can ignore the need to anticipate environmental discontinuities and that goes far beyond simply complying with regulations. The question: What if the way we operate is made illegal?

Technology

Rapid advances in technology have had, and are having, a more profound impact on organizations than any of the other factors considered in this book. Every aspect of a company is being transformed. Relationships with suppliers, employees, customers and regulators are being manged by rapidly evolving digital means. Platform businesses like Airbnb, Autotrader, Rightmove and Uber have radically upended traditional busines models. The volume of data now available to understand customer behaviour and the communications channels used to build an enduring relationship with them has created an entire new mind-set in marketing.

Many of the current generation of board directors started out working in organizations where the discussion of technology was limited to decisions about which computer system to buy and the IT department was seen as a backroom support function. But now technology – in the sense of the digitisation of information - has, and continues to, transform all aspects of an operation. Technology, which once was controlled by somebody who reported to somebody who reported to the Finance Director is now a central boardroom issue.

The accounting function was digitised a long time ago – most people in the finance function cannot remember a world before spreadsheets. But now all parts of the business system have experienced digital transformation through the collecting and curating of huge data sets and the immediate transfer of information. Procurement is done in an on-line marketplace, customer relations are managed by email. HR teams use artificial intelligence to sort cv's and assess people for promotions.

Most companies were well aware of the potential of the internet in the 1990s but they did not see just how profound the impact would be by the 2010s – thus proving Amara's Law[5] which states "We tend

---

[5] Roy Charles Amara (7 April 1925 – 31 December 2007) President of the Institute for the Future

to overestimate the effect of a technology in the short run and underestimate the effect in the long run"

In boardrooms, now, in the 2020s the discussion will include the implications of robotics, machine learning, cybersecurity and data privacy. Broadly anything that can be automated will be. Directors know this but many boards are not acting fast enough to get ahead of the changes

A further complication is that radical change is often not a function of the application of one technology but a previously unexploited grouping. Uber – the ride hailing platform – only exists because of a combination of GPS (Global Positioning Satellites), Cell phone networks (4G) and the internet. And then the manifestation of all these in the Smartphone . No Smartphone – no Uber.

The challenge for a board is how to anticipate the impact of technology when most directors are not technologists. Anticipating technology advances is one of the more problematic What if…? Areas to address. Perhaps the question is: What if some technological advance could wholly replace part of our business system…what would that mean to us ?

Legislation And Regulation

Companies are forced to follow rules. Employment legislation, product standards, environmental controls. Some operate in regulated industries with controls on licensing , pricing and risk management. Boards have a legal obligation to understand and comply with regulations but they should also spend time evaluating likely legislative developments not just worrying about compliance.

The rules, of course, are constantly changing. But legislation and regulation is not always predictable. What starts as a few angry Tweets may escalate to protests in the street and might, one day, end up on the statute book. Regressive boards usually see changes in legislation as a threat and will lobby for status quo. Progressive boards will seek to get ahead by adopting new rules as company policy before the law arrives and by looking for ways the new regulations can be used to provide competitive advantage.

A board which plans to grow by making acquisitions will probably at some point run into the competition regulators who may wish to investigate or even block a proposed transaction. Rather than having to appoint lawyers and scramble around at the last moment a progressive board will have been working on making the economic and social case that its acquisition strategy is not against the public interest. They will have commissioned economic studies to define their market in a broad fashion and will have engaged with politicians and competition regulations well ahead of announcing any deal.

Much legislation is easy to predict. Taxes, worker protection and product safety standards rarely go down. The less easy to anticipate What If…questions are most likely to be something specific to a company's sector. For theatre operators, for example, a sudden set of rules responding to an accident might outlaw the use of drinks containers made of glass, or a require for a new high level of fire safety equipment or insist on a certain number of exits from an auditorium.

Boards need to engage with lobbyists and lawyers to game play what might happen rather than preparing only for what they hope or dread.

Employees

An inexorable trend is that employing people will get more expensive. Pensions, paid vacations, parental leave, sabbaticals, health and safety, minimum wages, employment taxes – are all going to increase. Companies need to find ways to produce more with fewer people. Directors need to investigate automation and outsourcing as well as general productivity improvements. As technology gets cheaper human input gets most costly.

Boards may agonize over the remuneration of C-suite executives and worry about shareholder reactions to overly generous CEO packages but do they spend enough time thinking about how to be a highly attractive place to work in the future for the scarce, and expensive, resource that is young people.

In the war for talent it is increasingly not just levels of wages that attract and retain the best its the broad package of work and, increasingly, the company's public image and ethical policies which are board level issues to control.

Before the Covid crisis Millennials and Gen Z workers had been pushing back against the 9to5 commuter lifestyle accepted by Baby Boomers and Gen X. Many new entrants to the workforce now shun traditional employers and are seeking to work for companies that demonstrate good corporate citizen credentials. Now that working from home has become established and acceptable and now that companies are being regularly held to account for polluting externalities and poor operating practices the board has a significant role in setting standards which will win plaudits from potential employees.

Ten years ago it would have been hard to imagine a board asking "What if the best people refuse to work in San Francisco" but that is now a reality. The exodus from Silicon Valley is well underway – the future is full of surprises.

MAKING IT HAPPEN

The central theme of this book is that boards should not just monitor performance but should combine executive and non-executive experience to invest time in discussing possible environmental changes , picking up weak signals, anticipating the future and mapping out a course of action to enable their organization to thrive. Boards need to be asking "What if...?" not just "Why ...? But of course seeing the opportunities and threats and making plans is still a very long way from actually getting things done. Change is hard to implement. There are legions of examples of a corporate leadership having the right insights, seeing what is needed and then the company fails to deliver.

Turning strategy into action is the role of management but the board has a role to play in devising and promoting the initiatives needed and then providing the resources and incentives to get the organization to endorse and support the plan. Inevitably addressing new opportunities will require changes to business as usual mind-set and process and most organizations are very resistant to this. The board must be a champion for change.

The barriers to implementation are various types of legacy. The more successful a company is the more the legacy acts as an anchor.

<u>Legacy Assets:</u> Retailers with lots of physical shops or newspaper publishers who own printing plants across the country are reluctant to consider a future where these assets have little value. When confronted with falling sales and profits there is a temptation to seek solutions which make better use of the legacy

assets rather than abandoning them. But that delays the inevitable and acts as a disincentive to invest in alternatives.

Legacy attitudes: Members of a board, as senior managers or non executives, can afford to consider a radically changed future for an organization but this is not so easy for most of the management and employees. I have a very clear recollection of being in a meeting of 100 or so senior and middle management of the local newspaper group I chaired who had watched a presentation about the threat of the internet. In the ensuing question and answer session one of the more long serving team members said that he knew the internet was likely to ruin local papers "… but that's a decade away and I am five years from retirement so I am happy to sit this out with things as they are" He got an enthusiastic round of applause and, of course, he was correct. For him the challenges of the future was not a problem in a time frame the would impact him. For his company it would be a catastrophe.

It is not only existing executives not wanting to change. The whole organization can be adverse to bringing in new skills such as digital marketing or e-commerce as they do not fit neatly into the current management structure and can be seen as threatening to long-standing managers. There will be a tendency to try to repurpose exiting departments and retrain existing staff rather than make them redundant and bring in outsiders.

Legacy shareholders: Professional investors – asset managers – have different objectives. Some want to be paid dividends, others seek capital growth. A company which feels it must change direction can encounter shareholder resistance. When I was Chairman of Future, the magazine publisher, we wanted to stop paying dividends to invest in digital content but one of our large shareholders threatened various reprisals if we did. They ran a yield fund which needed dividends to meet its promises.

Ideally they would have sold their shares and invested in a different company but they did not want to book a loss on their position – they remained holders and lobbied for no change in policy. It held the company back.

Boards should not be involved in day-to-day management but they do have devices which can be used to encourage the implementation of change programmes. The board can take steps to create an environment in which change is easier to achieve. It can be seen to back initiatives which support the executive directors and reinforce the need to address future opportunities and threats. Board actions include:

Requesting Project Timetables: A board can ask for a clear set of milestones and objectives for one or more change projects and request regular reports. Senior management will all be aware that the milestones are being monitored by the board.

Creating Incentives: Management bonuses can be linked to achieving specific desired changes. Boards need to identify metrics to assess the degree of organizational support for and alignment with the actions they feel must be made. Executives should report on, and be incentivised, to achieve these metrics.

Encourage "Skunk Works": This is the idea pioneered by aircraft maker Lockheed Martin to locate radical projects in a specific location with a separate team away from the main business (they took their name from a cartoon series). Boards can approve a budget for special projects and locations to be established.

External Communication: A board can make public commitments on an initiative which is then known to the whole organization and becomes a visible part of the company mission. With a public goal in place it adds momentum to internal efforts.

A key role for the board is to have a thought through Plan B ready to go. Plan A is, in practice, executing business-as-usual. This is the activity described in he annual budget and three year plan. The normal day to day actions to maximise sales, reduce costs and improve the quality of earnings.

Plan B is what you do if some of the bigger "What Ifs…" come to fruition. Rather than having emergency meetings about what do when an event occurs Plan B is ready to swing into action. The more obvious examples are: interest rates suddenly go up or down by 3 or 4 % points; there is another oil price shock; the CEO or CFO walks out or is forced to quit; emergency legislation in effect bans or restrict your core products from sale. A competitor files for bankruptcy.

Executing the change initiatives will often require a reduction or cessation in BaU activity such as merging department or closing office locations . This will be met with resistance. The board can help by developing and by being seen to support a clear narrative about what the changes are vital.

CONCLUSIONS

I started this book by comparing the fortunes of two publishing companies: Future, which has thrived, and Johnston which has not. In the context of this book, I would describe the board of Future having been at the "progressive" end of the spectrum and that of Johnston as having been more in the "regressive" mould. The Future board asked itself how publishing would change with the arrival of the internet and looked at ways their business should adapt. The Johnston board saw the internet as a threat and decided to invest in protecting its (very successful and admired) established business model.

It is all too easy to make this analysis and classification with hindsight but looking back like this does offer lessons for people on boards today. The main message of this book is that executives are doing their jobs well when they manage business-as-unusual and are mostly, and correctly, focused on short-term goals. Those same executives when they assume their director role join with non-executives to create a board. That board, in addition to its oversight and monitoing tasks, should actively discuss and anticipate events which may present both threats and opportunities. The board should be asking: What If…? not just "Why…?

The board of an organization has the legal responsibility to run it properly. Good boards ensure accurate reporting, demonstrate awareness of their company's environmental impact and social responsibility, and adhere to high standards of governance. Great boards go beyond business-as-usual to anticipate the potential for disruption. Successful companies are led by directors who encourage innovation and practice well researched risk taking.

This book has argued the most important board role is to develop an informed and consensus view about what the future holds and ensure the organization is well prepared. Other points made in the text include:

- A company (be it profit seeking, public or private or a not-for profit) is a group of individuals who work together for a common goal - typically but not always to create wealth and deliver services. Their mission goes beyond making a profit.
- The late 20th century notion of a company being run solely to generate wealth for its shareholders is now broadly rejected as directors accept that a company has to be a good corporate citizen and balance the needs of a wider group of stakeholders.
- Directors have a responsibility to think about how to navigate the range of future events not just oversee day-to-day operations.
- Boards talk about managing risk, try to quantify it and have contingency plans. But they should also be discussing how to respond to uncertainty and opportunity.
- A risk register is a good start to identify potential problems and formally describe mitigating actions but it is only part of the story. A classic risk-register is focused on the downside and does not prompt discussions about opportunities. It can inhibit innovation. If process gets too formalised it can become more of a corporate ritual to produce text for the annual report rather than a real discussion of challenges.
- Progressive boards are curious about the future and open to new ideas. Regressive boards feel their existing business model and approach is the right one and tend to reject new thinking
- The organization's stakeholders all have their own agendas and their own objectives and whilst it is unlikely that any of

them will want the organization to fail they are each focused on their own desired outcomes: The board cannot please them all.
- Professional investors managing pension funds and the like can become too focused on earnings and dividend performance and not ask enough questions about how a company is positioned for the future. Boards need to have a convincing and informed narrative about their plans.
- To anticipate the future with success boards need diversity of experience. This partly comes from seeking a gender balance and BAME membership but it is mostly achieved by picking directors who are not cut from the same cloth as the executives. Diversity of experience thinking is the objective. Boards are not a representative democracy.
- The budgeting and planning processes are largely an extrapolation of current trends. They are not so much anticipation of the future as simple maths. Anticipation is a non-linear assessment if the sort of events which might turn up as surprises.
- It can be irritating and distracting if during a board meeting a director wants to pose "what if...?" questions but as long as a balance is maintained with the normal board duties it is these discussions which help a company both avoid the worst problems and, even more importantly, be ready for the big opportunities.

Companies like AirBnB, Amazon, Tesla and Uber worth billions when many hotel, retail and automotive firms are struggling. The argument in this book is because their boards manage for the future which they did not see as a linear extension of the past.

The next ten years, the 2020s, the post-Covid decade will see more disruption than any of todays generation of board directors has experienced before. The advances in technology, particularly artificial intelligence and robotics, will be even more rapid; the radical measures forced by climate change will dramatically affect the way corporation operate. The lengthy Covid lockdowns will lead to a fundamental revision of the ideas about work/offices/commuting and the way cities function. Boards will not be able to reply on past experience they will need to think about how to navigate uncertainty.

Successful companies, be they commercial or not-for-profit, usually become winners because of great management. Executing well, getting things done, having high energy and dedication are the main ingredients of corporate champions. This short book has been about the role of the board in giving a company a clear sense of direction. I am not suggesting, in any way, that the board plays a more important role than the executives. Far from it. The argument is that poor boards, regressive boards, can hold the company back by focusing on the wrong things. Even boards comprised of outstanding individuals can develop bad habits as a group. If you are a member of a board ask the question of your fellow directors: "Are we running this organization by looking back in the rear view mirror or forward through the windscreen? Are we anticipating disruption?"

Acknowledgements

I have been a member of more than 30 boards and have been Chairman of 17. As a result I have been on boards with more than 100 people acting as directors and I think it is fair to say I have learned lessons from all of them. Everyone brings something to the board table and I am now firmly convinced that the most effective boards comprise directors (executive and non-executive) with a broad range of experience. To name all my fellow directors, to whom I owe a debt of gratitude, would be a challenge and as some of my boards go back to the early days of the internet not easy to recall every name but I would like to offer a collective "thank you" for the insights and the entertainment.

I have been fortunate that some of the boards I have been on controlled companies which have thrived so there is a collective sense of achievement. I have also been Chairman of two that went into administration on my watch and a couple which subsequently went under so I am in no position to claim an unblemished track record. But all of them – the successes and the failures – bring insights.

The argument is this book has been that boards, more than anything, should anticipate - look forwards. Other people may well argue boards should have different priorities but this approach comes directly from my own experiences. The companies I was on, which enjoyed the greatest economic success, include Future (magazine publishing), More Group (out of home advertising), YouGov (data analysis). In all cases those boards regularly discussed what our industry would look like five years hence and how we could be a successful part of that future.

In terms of education I should also say that the various CEOs and CFOs I have been privileged to work with are a huge source of learning. Some executives regard the board as a nuisance which slows down decision making and is risk averse but the best ones use the board as a forum to test out ideas and use the non-executives as a safe surrogate for understanding the likely views of various stakeholders. The best boards really do exhibit teamwork.

There is no right answer as to how to chair a board. I hope this short book is a useful contribution to the debate.

Author Biography

Roger Parry is the charman of two public companies Oxford Metrics plc and YouGov plc and is a non-executive director of Uber in the UK. He was, amongst others, Chairman of: Clear Channel International, Future Publishing, Johnston Press, MSQ Partners and Shakespeare's Globe. He has been an executive at Aegis, More Group, McKinsey & Co and WCRS. He was a broadcaster at the BBC, ITV and LBC. Educated at the universities of Oxford and Bristol. Appointed CBE for services to media in 2014.

Cover Photograph: This book is a product of the Covid crisis. I found myself locked down in the Bahamas for a couple of months. The photograph on the cover of the paperback edition is the view from my office on a stormy morning. It turned out to be a lovely day.

Printed in Great Britain
by Amazon